*The
Disappearance
of Snow*

## Also by Manuel Rivas

*Poems*
Libro do Entroido
Balada nas praias do Oeste
Mohicania
Ningún cisne
Costa da Morte Blues
O pobo da noite
Do descoñecido ao descoñecido
A desaparición da neve

*in English*
From Unknown to Unknown

*Novels, short stories and plays*
Todo ben
Un millón de vacas
Os comedores de patacas
En salvaxe compaña
Que me queres, amor?
Bala perdida
O lapis do carpinteiro
Ela, maldita alma
A man dos paíños
As chamadas perdidas
Contos de Nadal
Os libros arden mal
Todo é silencio
O máis estraño
O heroe (play)

*in English*
The Carpenter's Pencil
Butterfly's Tongue
Vermeer's Milkmaid
In the Wilderness
Books Burn Badly

# The Disappearance of Snow

*A desaparición da neve*

# Manuel Rivas

*Translated by*
*Lorna Shaughnessy*

Shearsman Books

First published in the United Kingdom in 2012 by
Shearsman Books
50 Westons Hill Drive
Emersons Green
Bristol
BS16 7DF

Shearsman Books Ltd Registered Office
30–31 St. James Place, Mangotsfield, Bristol BS16 9JB
(this address not for correspondence)

http://www.shearsman.com/

ISBN 978-1-84861-221-1

Original poems copyright © 2009, Manuel Rivas
Translations copyright © 2012, Lorna Shaughnessy
Introduction copyright © 2012, Martín Veiga

The right of Manuel Rivas to be identified as the author of this work and of Lorna Shaughnessy to be identified as the translator thereof has been asserted by them in accordance with the Copyrights, Designs and Patents Act of 1988.
All rights reserved.

This volume is published by arrangement with Literarische Agentur Mertin Inh. Nicole Witt e. K., Frankfurt, Germany. The original text was published by Santillana Ediciones, Madrid, in 2009.

**Acknowledgements**
Grateful acknowledgement is made to the editors of *Cyphers* magazine in which a number of these translations first appeared. I am especially grateful to Jonathan Dunne for his encouragement and support of this project, and to Professor Diarmuid Bradley and Dr Mel Boland for their indispensable soundings.

Thanks to Manus Walsh for permission to reproduce his painting 'Between Earth and Sea' on the cover.

# Contents

| | |
|---|---:|
| Introduction | 9 |
| A enigmática organización | |
|     The Enigmatic Order | 19 |
| Herba do cego | |
|     Blind Man's Grass | 23 |
| Meu amor puxo unha bomba do baleiro | |
|     My Love is a Suction-Force Pump | 25 |
| Meu amor contrabandista | |
|     My Smuggler Love | 29 |
| Cantiga de amor | |
|     Cantiga de amor | 33 |
| O monte do faro | |
|     Lighthouse Hill | 35 |
| O retorno | |
|     The Homecoming | 39 |
| Manifesto | |
|     Manifesto | 41 |
| A panadeira de Ingres | |
|     Ingres and the Baker's Daughter | 47 |
| Oes chegar Ángel González? | |
|     Waiting for Ángel González | 49 |
| A rosa invisíbel | |
|     The Invisible Rose | 51 |
| A meiga na esquina da barra | |
|     The Witch in the Corner of the Bar | 53 |
| Vento tehuelche | |
|     Tehuelche Wind | 55 |
| Enterro campesiño | |
|     Country Burial | 57 |
| Castro Laboreiro | |
|     Castro Laboreiro | 59 |

Graffiti
    Graffiti    61
Metamorfose
    Metamorphosis    63
Vangarda
    Vanguard    65
Espiritual
    Spiritual    67
Resurrección
    Resurrection    69
Terminus
    Terminus    71
Historia do silencio
    A History of Silence    73
Historia da arte
    A History of Art    77
Historia do diñeiro
    A History of Money    81
A man baleira (11-M)
    The Empty Hand (11-M)    87
Vieira pop-art
    Scallop Pop-Art    89
O canon
    The Canon    91
Tons de gris baixo o ceo
    Shades of Grey under the Sun    93
Unha chamada perdida
    Missed Call    97
Boh
    Boh    101
Mayday
    Mayday    105
O subtraccionismo
    Taking Stock    111

Así se fai un poeta
    How to Make a Poet    113
O valor das cousas
    The Value of Things    115
Alalá
    Alalá    117
Guia práctica
    A Practical Guide    119
Toque de oración
    Call to Prayer    121
Terra de fogo
    Tierra del Fuego    125
Ósos e tellas
    Bones and Roof-Tiles    127
O corvo de Noé
    Noah's Raven    129

Notes / Glossary    130

# Snow, Memory and the Angel of History: Manuel Rivas at the Crossroads

## Martín Veiga

Poetry has the power to reveal what lies buried underneath the surface of things, it allows us to penetrate through that surface and to explore the dark depths of the unknown, as if breaking a blanket of ice on a lake in midwinter. For Manuel Rivas, the act of writing implies a journey into the unknown, the inquiry into the enigmas of being, a constantly renewed act of faith in the healing possibilities of language. Poetry is for Rivas the mother cell from which all his writing emerges. Everything he writes, be it his internationally acclaimed works of fiction or his essays and journalism, emanates from the seed of his poetic mind. Poetry is the core and the protein of Rivas's writing. Poetry is the root that travels deep into the unknown but grows many different leaves out of that darkness, following a process evoked by Yeats in 'The Coming of Wisdom with Time', a poem that Rivas knows well and is very fond of: "Though leaves are many, the root is one". His work is profoundly rooted in his immediate experience and therefore exhibits both an acute sense of place and a clear awareness of history and tradition, but it also epitomises the increasing levels of presence, visibility and projection of Galician culture in the global context. In this respect, Rivas has contributed greatly to the flourishing and consolidation of literature in Galician worldwide in recent years, and he has authored some of Galicia's most widely translated books, some of which have received prestigious awards and have been successfully adapted into films.

*The Disappearance of Snow* was first published in Spain in 2009, in a striking multilingual edition which included, in the same volume, the Galician original version together with Catalan, Basque and Castilian translations. Rivas argued that this initiative sought to create a space of dialogue or, using his own words, "a forest of biodiversity" for the different languages spoken in Spain, in an attempt to remove the ongoing social and political emphasis laid on linguistic conflict and to generate a greater recognition of the richness of linguistic plurality as a wealth that should be treasured. He insisted on these views in his speech of admission to the Real Academia Galega in December 2009, in which he defined memory, ecology and language as the driving forces of his literary discourse.

In this collection, and more generally throughout all of his creative and journalistic work, dichotomies such as the interaction between past and present, the coexistence of urban and rural cultures in Galicia, the conflicts between progress and tradition, the ebbs and flows of social history and personal emotion, reoccur often and in different forms. In a literary universe that attempts to address such paradoxical questions, it should not come as a surprise that the opening epigraph of *The Disappearance of Snow* is extracted from the poem 'A Song of Opposites' by John Keats: "And hear a merry laugh amid the thunder". Indeed, Rivas's work could also be described as a literary project that invariably proposes a concurrence of opposites.

The book is written on a mantle of snow beneath which the dormant memory of spring remains hidden. According to Rivas, the act of writing consists of a thaw that unearths a new world, so it is the disappearance of snow that generates this miracle. These poems are glittering gems found among the blizzard. In his poetry, language has the potential to restore what has been taken away, words return to summon what humanity has been deprived of: "Words come to reclaim what is theirs,/ all that was taken from them" ["Veñen as palabras reclamar o seu,/o subtraído"]. Antonio Machado had a similar intuition in one of the poems dedicated to his beloved Guiomar: "One sings what one loses" ["Se canta lo que se pierde"]. Memory is gradually restored through the active intervention of language, which thus becomes a crucial agent in the process of recovery of both individual and collective memory. It is a literary process which also has relevant ideological implications, particularly in light of recent political debates about the treatment of historical memory in Spain. In this regard, *The Disappearance of Snow* brings together personal and social memory, the public and the private, both of equal importance for Rivas, because, as he wrote in one of his newspaper articles, "we are what we remember" ["somos lo que recordamos"].

At the heart of the collection, personal memory shines with special intensity in love poems such as 'My Love is a Suction-Force Pump' ['Meu amor puxo unha bomba do baleiro'], 'My Smuggler Love' ['Meu amor contrabandista'] and 'Cantiga de amor'. These poems articulate the experience of love from multiple perspectives but, more importantly, they break down the conventional rhetoric of love and expand it in many directions in order to create a verbal waterfall of associated meanings. The narrative development of these texts takes the winding roads of imagination and the association of ideas as core cohesive elements, as occurs with other poems in which communication, or rather the realisation of its apparent impossibility, becomes the central theme. This motif, which may be identified in poems such as 'Missed Call' ['Unha chamada perdida'] and 'Mayday', resonates in other books of poetry and prose by Rivas, as exemplified by the telephone conversation poems in *Ningún cisne* and his short story collection *As chamadas perdidas*, whose revealing title suggests notions of loss, loneliness and failed communication.

History pervades *The Disappearance of Snow* and the poetic voice, transfixed as Walter Benjamin's angel of history, looks at the storm of progress, always moving between the horrors of the past and the uncertainties of a future that has yet to be written. However, for Rivas history does not mean an epic account of the grand events but rather the impact of those events on the oppressed and on the humble, such as in the poem 'A History of Money' ['Historia do diñeiro']: "My cap, on the ground, is the European Bank./Please don't throw your sadness in it." ["O meu sombreiro, no chan da rúa, é o banco de Europa./Por favor, non guindedes tristura no meu pucho"].

Unlike in Wallace Stevens's poem 'The Snow Man', one does not need to have a mind of winter to regard the snow thawing in this book as the ultimate manifestation of hope in humankind, even in a world dominated by hopelessness and fear. As a meditation on the illuminating power of memory and the acceptance of difference, this book is incisive, compassionate, humorous and deeply democratic. Harold Bloom once portrayed Ralph Waldo Emerson as a man whose tireless mind was always at some crossroads. *The Disappearance of Snow* represents the poetic crossroads where Manuel Rivas is standing, looking back towards the rubble of the past but always willing to move forward, merrily laughing amid the thunder, always ready to fly into the storm.

*For Diarmuid, Mel and all my colleagues.*

And hear a merry laugh amid the thunder

John Keats
*A Song of Opposites*

# A desaparición da neve

The Disappearance of Snow

# A enigmática organización

*A Marcos Valcárcel*

Veñen as palabras reclamar o seu,
o subtraído.
            Fóra dos campos de traballo,
móvense coidadosas como a porcelana
ou o primeiro día de abril.
Non osmas o recendo higrófilo
das súas follas de espiga,
a suor argonauta do seu gran?
Existen.
Existe o aviador que le braille na noite.
Existe a vesga que leva voces baixas
no seu paxe de ourizos.
Existe a boca da literatura,
a tola que fala soa
como unha medusa.
Existe a boca do pozo que enxamea,
polposa, mal falada,
protexendo os seus.
Existe outra saudade.
Existe o tren onde viaxa unha saudade
desposuída.
Dormen as palabras
baixo o alzheimer das pontes.
Nos sumidoiros desenvólvese a historia:
as falsas testemuñas torturan os poemas.
No tormento da asfixia,
perden o ar,
a valiosa información.
Salvaranse os que simulen a morte
nun esplendor de herba.
Ou os que lembren un romance de cego

# The Enigmatic Order

*For Marcos Valcárcel*

Words come to reclaim what is theirs,
all that was taken from them.
        Outside the labour camps
they move, tentative as porcelain
or the first day of April.
Can't you smell the hydrophilic scent
of their leaves of maize,
the argonaut sweat of their grain?
They exist.
Exist like the aviator who reads braille at night.
Exist like the cross-eyed woman who carries hushed voices
in her basket of sea-urchins.
Exist in the mouth of literature,
the madwoman who talks to herself
like a medusa.
Exist like the seething mouth of the well,
viscous, foul-mouthed,
protective of its own.
Exist like another kind of longing.
Like the train where a dispossessed yearning
journeys into exile.
Words sleep
beneath Alzheimer bridges.
In the sewers history unfolds:
false witnesses torture poems.
In the torment of asphyxiation
they lose air,
the prized information.
They will be saved only if they play dead
on a blaze of grass.
Or remember a blind man's ballad

onde todo se conta
sen esperanza e sen medo.
Ou aqueles que rescate a enigmática organización
das palabras en vilo.

where everything is told
without hope and without fear.
Or salvage the enigmatic order
of words that catch fire, mid air.

# Herba do cego

A Poussin, o normando,
pedíronlle o agasallo máis fermoso
do mundo antigo
para un museo de Roma.
Non perdeu unha hora.
Elixiu unha presa de terra.
Esa materia estraña,
esa masa de sombras
que leveda coa aurora.
Un puñado de terra,
unha cotra de sangue,
unha pútrida alma
salgada
co po de mármore das estatuas.
Unha presa de terra,
un rescaldo de invernos,
o mundo antigo a soñar
na elevación da estruga,
da herba de cego,
no molde dunha man.

# Blind Man's Grass

They asked Poussin, the Norman,
to select the most beautiful gift
from the ancient world
for a museum in Rome.
It didn't even take an hour.
He chose a handful of earth,
that strange matter,
a mass of shadows
that ferments with each dawn.
A handful of earth,
a bloody scab,
a decomposing soul
seasoned
with the marble dust of statues.
A handful of earth,
embers of many winters,
an ancient world that dreams
of the elevation of the nettle,
blind man's grass
in the mould of a hand.

# Meu amor puxo unha bomba do baleiro

Meu amor ama as ferraxarías.
Que ollas, meu amor?
Unha bomba do baleiro.
Celebraremos o noso aniversario
cunha bomba aspirante e impelente,
incesante,
aspirante e impelente,
incesante.
Percorreremos o álbum de familia
cun detector de metais.
Un amor incrustado,
soterrado,
arqueolóxico.
Un anaco cego de lóstrego
entobado.
Meu amor ama o lignito,
a turba das linguas mortas,
a grama que espiga nos dentes,
as plantas industriais,
as explotacións a ceo aberto.
Unha bomba para baleirar o baleiro.
Meu amor ama as ferramentas
de cavar baixo a chuvia.
Hai tres mil anos labrei para ti
esa peza de ouro,
esa ave que foxe,
a escaleira que descende
ao fondo da botella.
Meu amor traballa os días todos,
todo o día traballa meu amor.
Os días de festa traballa
como un himno traballa meu amor.

# My Love Is a Suction-Force Pump

My love is a lover of hardware stores.
What are you looking at, my love?
A vacuum pump.
Let's celebrate our anniversary
with a suction-force pump,
suction, release
suction, release
non-stop.
Let's scan the family album
with a metal detector.
An embedded love,
subterranean,
archaeological.
A fragment of lightning
blind in its mine-shaft.
My love is a lover of lignite,
the peat of dead tongues,
the grass that sprouts between teeth,
industrial plants,
open-cast mines.
A vacuum pump to empty out the void.
My love is a lover of tools
for digging in the rain.
Three thousand years ago I crafted for you
that piece of gold,
the bird that flees,
the stairs that descend
to the bottom of the bottle.
My love works every day,
all day long my love works.
Even on feast days,
like a hymn, my love is working.

É un corpo misterioso, meu amor.
Todo xira no xiro da súa saia.
Como a pel do trompetista,
nada se pousa na súa suor.
Entrou no videoxogo
ía ofrecida á Virxe, meu amor,
a disparar cravos pola boca,
esa é a forza que temos,
o espírito,
o cuspe que anavalla,
o gume de Deus.
Que ben sae da aventura, meu amor.
Que ben fai o sitio.
Leva envolta unha glicinia.
Sen acougo, bombea flor.
Fai transfusións de nubes.
Todo o crea,
todo o destrúe,
meu amor.
Vai poñendo bombas no baleiro.
É dunha violencia suave
que desenterra aves nas enxivas
cabalos do hipocampo,
por aí non, meu amor,
non me desenterres por aí,
por aí si,
baixo o concheiro,
baixo as aras,
baixo as armas,
baixo a inscrición borrada,
no inaccesíbel,
pon unha bomba aí,
no inaccesíbel.
E ti, rocha da tristeza, aparta.
Aparta que todo o destrúe
meu amor.

A mysterious body, is my love.
Everything swirls around her swirling skirt.
Like the trumpet-player's skin,
nothing settles on her sweat.
She went into videogames,
offered up to the Virgin, my love,
shooting nails from her mouth,
that's the power we have,
the spirit,
the spit that slits,
the knife-edge of God.
She was made for adventure, my love.
No-one can lay a siege like her.
She carries concealed wisteria,
tirelessly pumping flowers.
She makes cloud transfusions.
Creates everything
destroys everything,
my love.
Off she goes, installing vacuum pumps in the void.
Hers' is a tender violence
that releases birds in the mouth,
horses in the hippocampus
not here, my love,
don't dig me up here,
over there,
under the shell-heap
under altars
under coats of arms
under the faded inscription,
in the unreachable,
put a pump there
in the unreachable.
And you, rock of sorrow, can stand aside.
Stand aside because everything will be destroyed
by my love.

# Meu amor contrabandista

Meu amor anda ás crebas pola beiramar.
Vai preñada de vento,
vai preñada de néboa,
do lóstrego vai,
todo o apaña
apáñao todo
coa luz beatísima do seu vesgo ollar.
O ben que leva co temporal,
como o amansa,
24 fotogramas por minuto,
a dureza mística,
a luz facinorosa
do seu pestanexar.
E el dálle zapatos sempre do mesmo pé,
o andar dos deuses
coxos do mar.
Meu amor enche o ventre
de seixos silábicos,
de runas, de aghoams,
de voces baixas,
pictogramas coprófagos
que crían nos excrementos da lúa.
Meu amor anda ás crebas pola beira da esfera,
nas estradas solitarias,
no ceo dos manequíns
onde rompen as nubes,
nos cemiterios dos pingüíns xigantes
cos seus portafolios de naturezas mortas.
Vai preñada por dentro,
cara a dentro,
como unha guía en tempo de éxodo.
Ese ollar delincuente,

# My Smuggler-Love

My love is out scouring beaches.
There she goes, pregnant with wind,
pregnant with fog,
with lightening,
grabbing everything for herself,
for herself, every thing
by the most holy light of her squinty eye.
See how well she weathers the storm,
how she calms it,
24 frames per minute,
the austere revelation,
the delinquent light
of her every blink.
And it gives her shoes, always for the same foot,
the lame gait
of sea-gods.
My love fills her womb
with syllabic shingle,
with runes, ogham stones,
hushed voices,
coprophagus pictographs
hatched in the moon's faeces.
My love is out scouring the rim of the globe,
down lonely roads
in model skies
where clouds disperse,
in the burial grounds of giant penguins
with their portfolios of stilled lives.
She is pregnant inside,
looking inwards,
like a guide in a time of exodus.
With her delinquent's eyes,

ese corpo de contrabandista de seda,
esa voz rouca.
Durmía cos ollos abertos meu amor.
Non sei vivir
sen o rumor do seu vesgo ollar.
Meu amor anda ás crebas na noite.
Apaña os restos aleixoados
do ben e do mal,
un cargamento ultramarino de esdrúxulas,
un fardo de cousas septiformes,
o contedor de frascos de potencias da alma.
Veni Sancte Spiritus,
meu amor atopou o bébedo Xonás.
Meu amor di que Xonás era el o gran peixe.
Xonás preñado de seu,
de abismo.
Meu amor funde os pés na area,
leva no ventre un arfar canso de nai virxe,
un canto de gorxa inuit,
o nome impronunciábel do mesmo temporal.
Meu amor vai parindo de pé
o poema da illa.
Cercada polas ondas,
o corpo aberto,
a ollada fértil,
as mans vesgas
a amasar,
a levedar o tempo petrificado.
Et tui amoris in eis ignem accende
and kindle in them the fire of thy love.
Meu amor enténdese co mar,
ese fillo de puta,
meu amor.

her silken smuggler's body,
her husky voice.
My love used to sleep with her eyes open.
And I don't know how to live
without the sound of her squinty eye.
My love is out combing beaches all night.
She salvages the maimed remains
of good and evil,
a shipment of accented words,
a bale of seven-sided things,
a container of jars of the soul's potential.
Veni Sancte Spiritus,
My love met the drunken Jonah.
My love says Jonah was the big fish.
Jonah, pregnant with himself,
with the abyss.
My love sinks her feet in the sand,
carries in her womb a virgin mother's quick breath,
an Inuit throat-song,
the unpronounceable name of the storm itself.
My love stands on her own two feet and gives birth
to the poem of the island.
Hemmed in by waves,
open-bodied,
fertile-eyed,
fingers splayed
to knead
fermenting, petrified time.
Et tui amoris in eis ignem accende
and kindle in them the fire of thy love.
My love sees eye-to-eye with the sea,
that son of a bitch,
my love.

# Cantiga de amor

Moveranse os corpos
como maquis
polos lindes da noite.
Entrarán nadando o un no outro,
Mia Senhor,
como outrora entrou a fame na Galiza.

# Cantiga de amor

Their bodies will move
like partisans,
skirting the perimeters of the night,
swimming into one another,
my love,
the way famine came to Galicia.

# O monte do faro

*A Maria Rivas Barros, in memoriam*

Oes o traballo da luz?
O seu punzón de tipógrafo,
o imprentar o invisíbel nos espellos,
o chío da hora azul
a morrer na deshora?

Teño na boca
vinte e seis millas de luz.
Nas faltas dos dentes,
a dor da luz.

Oes o traballo secreto da luz?
Oes a fatiga sentinela,
o remoer da vixía?
O bruar da luz,
os pasos cegos da luz no herbal neboento,
a espallar o rescaldo dos ósos dos soños?

A vinte e seis millas de luz
navegan os mortos
que non queren ser tristes.
Andan polo mar ás ceibas,
o andar de Charlot,
cunha bandeira de 26 millas náuticas de luz.

Os nenos de Monte Alto
ollan polo ollo da caveira
o escaravello de ouro de Allan Poe
        — *Poe, poe, poe!*
náufrago nun sombreiro
dun gángster devoto e dadaísta.

# Lighthouse Hill

*In memoriam María Rivas Barrós*

Can you hear the working of the light?
Its typographer's punch-cutter
printing the invisible onto mirrors,
the chirruping of the twilight hour
as it dies late in the evening?

I have in my mouth
twenty-six miles of light.
In the gaps of missing teeth,
the pain of light.

Can you hear the secret working of the light?
Can you hear its watchful fatigue,
the spy's mind at work?
The roaring of the light,
the blind footsteps of light in furrows of fog,
spreading the dung of dreams?

Twenty-six miles of light from here
the dead with no wish to be sad
set sail.
They step freely onto the sea,
walking like Chaplin,
carrying a flag of twenty-six nautical miles of light.

The children of Monte Alto
peep through the skull's eye
at Allan Poe's gold bug
     — *Poe, poe, poe!*
marooned in the hat
of an inveterate, Dadaist gangster.

Oes o traballo da luz?
O asmático alampar,
os seus pés prendidos nas correas das algas luminarias,
as onomatopeas somnámbulas no odre dos ventos.
Oes o xuramentos ebrios dos afogados na taberna do mar,
oes o naipe da luz matar o tres?
Oes o seu rir de peixe de Caxemira
ao paso de El-Rei?
O seu ulululú de curuxa mariña,
o seu xxxxsssssss de narval,
a súa branca sombra cuspindo fósforo?

Oes o bisbar saprófito da luz?
Óelo levedar na noite de San Xoán,
as raíces ledas da podremia da luz,
a luz a brincar na aurora,
a revellida aurora,
a luz a vomitar
pequenos reloxos nas ambulancias?
Oes nos quirófanos
as ás da luz
os ovos negros da luz?

Oes o zunido da luz?
Oes como o arqueiro zen
sobe os chanzos
da col solitaria,
o tensar do seu arco,
a lenta frecha
que xa vén,
que atina en min, en min?

Oes o sangue da escuridade,
o esnacar dos seus ósos,
a luxación da noite,
o esmuxicar do mar,
o inmenso boi que brúa co teu pranto,
o pestanexo fero dos seus ollos pequenos?

Can you hear the working of the light?
Its asthmatic illumination,
its feet imprisoned in bonds of luminous seaweed,
the somnambulant onomatopoeias in the winds' wineskin?
Can you hear the drunken oaths of the drowned in the sea's tavern?
Can you hear the light as it plays the trump card?
Can you hear it laugh like the fish of Kashmir
when the King passes by,
its sea owl to-wit to-woo,
its narwhal whoosh,
its white shadow spitting phosphorous?

Can you hear the saprophytic murmurings of the light?
Can you hear it fermenting on St John's Eve,
the giddy roots of rotting light,
light that jumps over the bonfire of dawn,
the aging dawn,
light that spews up
small clocks in ambulances.
Can you hear its wings
in operating theatres,
its black eggs of light?

Can you hear the humming of the light?
Can you hear how the Zen archer
climbs the steps
of the solitary knoll,
draws back his bow,
the slow arrow
coming closer
and closer, piercing now?

Can you hear the blood in the darkness,
the breaking of bones,
the dislocated night,
the burning of the sea,
the huge ox that bellows with your grief
the wild blinking of its insignificant eyes?

# O retorno

*A Lois Pereiro*

En Itaca estaban todos mortos.
Dis que fun eu, Argos, o can, o primeiro en espertar:
—*Dead, dead, dead!*
Un cheiro máis forte que o do esterco,
o do home vivo,
foi o que me fixo vomitar os despoxos celestes,
os ósos das nubes,
os coiros do arco iris.
Aquel home que fedía a lenda,
con acenos de esqueleto incómodo
e espectro irado,
fendeu as unllas na cicatriz
e untou as sombras de lama das palabras.
Alí estaban os nosos nomes todos.
Tamén a memoria certeira das árbores
na horta de Laertes.
Medio cento de ringleiras de vides,
as trece pereiras,
as dez maceiras,
as corenta figueiras.
O vello cego viu, á fin, o fillo coa álxebra da terra.
Despois Odiseo
foinos espertando un a un
e as nosas bágoas son, dende entón,
o visgo que apreixa a luz
cunha violenta felicidade.

# The Homecoming

*For Lois Pereiro*

In Ithaca everyone was dead.
They say it was me, Argos the dog, who woke first:
    — *Dead, dead, dead!*
A smell stronger than dung,
the smell of a living man,
made me vomit celestial remains,
cloud-bones,
rainbow-hides.
That man who reeked of legend,
a twitching skeleton,
a bad-tempered ghost,
ripped open the scar with his nails
and smeared the mired shadows with words.
There were our names. All of them.
And the infallible memory of the trees
in Laertes' orchard.
Half a hundred rows of vines,
thirteen pear trees,
ten apple trees,
forty fig trees.
The blind old man saw, in the end, his son, thanks to the earth's
    algebra.
After, Odysseus
came and woke us one by one
and our tears, since then,
are the rope that binds the light
with a violent joy.

# Manifesto

I

Nos fornos de pan,
con lume de uz,
o levedar a neve.

II

O que desaparece, o que esmorece e podrece,
os ollos voitres á procura da preada,
as poutas nas órbitas da resurrección.

III

Mais ás veces, si.
Os ollos escoitan o crepitar da lúa,
o folerpar inquieto das muxicas,
os pasos de quen regresa a un corpo.

IV

E toda esa resignación,
caido illó de herba
que o angazo apaña,
segue pensando en ti,
que empuñas a gadaña.

# Manifesto

I

In bread ovens
where heather burns,
the snow ferments.

II

All that disappears, all that fades and rots,
the buzzard's search for carrion,
its talons around resurrection's eyes.

III

But sometimes, it's true
that eyes can heed the crackling of the moon,
the unsettling snow of falling cinders,
the footsteps of someone returning to a body.

IV

And all that resignation,
like a swathe of cut grass
the rake clears away
keeps thinking of you,
who swings the scythe.

V

Bafo vacún do mar,
memoria crúa
que estra o seu sudario
polos sucos da noite
para estercar misterio.


VI

Á escura luz
do guizo,
da candea da uz,
ir ver de fóra dentro.


VII

Afunde, a unha distancia cómica,
o terror que marchou,
mentres enxamea
na liña tensa do mar
a estarrecedora saudade do que amei.


VIII

Na poza invernal, o arco da vella
é un divino óleo á altura dos pés.
Só falta un *valenthuomo* que escachice
o inaccesíbel.

V

The sea steams like cattle,
a raw memory
that spreads its shroud
along the night's furrows,
feeding mystery.


VI

By the dark light
of the date palm,
of the heather lantern,
go and see from the outside in.


VII

The terror that departed
sinks at a comic distance –
while on the sea's taut line
there teems
a cruel longing for all I loved.


VIII

In winter's chilly pool, the rainbow
is a divine oil painting at our feet.
All that's missing is a *valenthuomo* to shatter
the impenetrable.

IX

Oes o andantino do mar,
o allegrisimo?
Sobe, sobe polos chanzos
da escaleira de caracol
coa excitación
dunha chave prestada.


e X

Por aquí, por aquí,
di o río.
Pola ingua da pedra,
polo espectro do salmón,
polo rumor dos museos,
cara ao mar do Temerario de Turner
e a Estixia de Patinir.

IX

Can you hear the sea's andantino,
its allegrissimo?
Go up, go up the steps
of the spiral staircase
with the thrill
of a borrowed key.


and X

This way, this way
says the river.
Past the edge of the stone,
past the spectre of the salmon,
past the murmurings of museums,
towards the sea of Turner's Téméraire
and the river of Patinir's Styx.

# A panadeira de Ingres

*A Dios e a Perla*

A esa hora
séntese un corpo
feito de trapos vellos
con cotras de pigmentos,
palabras fanadas,
mans blasfemas,
cinzas de labaradas, decantacións,
sucos lacrimosos de cera,
o restroballo oleoso da poda de sombras,
o motín das cousas desprezadas,
as culpas amoreadas nas esquinas,
a escoura de trazos,
o intre tóxico, o sublime aleixoado,
o místico veleno,
a luz resentida no xacemento de espirais,
a empadumada do chan,
unha chaira de vento insomne,
ánimas dos morcegos nas pugas dos arames,
ovellas a roer o coiro das herbas,
a enigmática organización da néboa,
o malestar petrificado do destino,
o renxer da aurora florentina
na fiestra do estudio.
Á fin, Jean Ingres cede. Atrévese. Tensa o tremor.
Pinta as costas máis belas da historia dos corpos nus.
As de Margherita, filla do panadeiro Francesco Luti.
En 1518, Rafael Sanzio
dispense a agarimar aquela curva
e ela, a Fornarina,
sentada no regazo do pintor e amante,
olla a Ingres cun resplandor irónico de esposa,
ano de 1814.

# Ingres and the Baker's Daughter

*For Dios and Perla*

At that hour
you can just make out a figure
made of old rags
with incrustations of pigment,
amputated words,
blaspheming hands,
ashes of flames, decantings,
tear-like furrows of wax,
the oily residue of shadows made smaller,
the mutiny of scorned things,
guilt piled up in corners,
scuffed brushstrokes of paint,
the poisoned moment, the maimed sublime,
the mystical venom,
the reluctant light on spiralled deposits of paint,
the swamp that is the floor,
a flat expanse of sleepless wind,
souls of bats spiked on the barbed wire,
sheep that crop the leathery grasses,
the enigmatic order of the fog,
the petrified disquiet of fate,
the creaking open of the Florentine dawn
in the studio window.
Finally, Jean Ingres gives in. He dares. Steadies his hand.
Paints the most beautiful back in the history of the Nude.
It belongs to Margherita, daughter of the baker Francesco Luti.
In 1518, Raphael Sanzio
prepares to caress that curve
and she, la Fornarina,
from the lap of her painter-lover,
looks at Ingres with a wife's resplendent irony,
in the year 1814.

# Oes chegar Ángel González?

*Unha palabra e a seguinte déronme a terceira.*
                                        Edda Maior

O 11 de maio chegará ás praias
a primeira palabra
coas súas pisadas de nube con zancas.
Será levada polas tres mil tabernas
e tres librarías do Antigo Reino.
Será levada en vilo, aleluia,
e pasará o vao do río, aleluia,
alí onde sucumben
os árbitros de fútbol
e os oradores demasiado sobrios.
A segunda palabra
recibirémola dende o interior
e a aldraba no limiar
soará como o corazón dun xinete
cinguido aos ósos
cunha nobreza de briosa melancolía.
Traerá das asas
a maquinaria memorial do feitizo
coas súas teclas de carpíns brancos.
Ti, agora, deberías dicir a seguinte palabra.
Tela na punta da lingua.
Só co seu alento
prenderá un fósforo
e a lonxitude da flama
será a da túa vibración.

# Waiting for Ángel González

*One word and then the next gave me a third.*
            Elder Edda


On the eleventh of May
the first word
will arrive on the beaches,
striding like a long-legged cloud.
To be taken around the three thousand bars
and three bookshops of the Ancient Kingdom.
To be carried on high, alleluia,
across the ford of the river, alleluia,
to the place where football referees
and orators who are too serious
always back down.
The second word
will come to us inside
and the knocker on the front door
will pound like the heart of a rider
that clings to his ribs
with a spirited, sad dignity.
It will bring firmly in its grasp
the workings of memory's spell
with its white-socked letters.
And now it's up to you to say the next word.
You have it on the tip of your tongue.
Only your breath
can light the match
and its flame will burn
as long as life vibrates in you.

# A rosa invisíbel

Envexa do vento
que alporiza os cabelos
e abanea as saias,
o borboriño estampado,
das dúas mulleres no campo das gramíneas.
Envexa do papel en que todo está pintado,
desa rosa invisíbel
que incendia a sombra
e desfai os peiteados.

# The Invisible Rose

Envy the wind
that ruffles hair
and lifts skirts,
the patterned murmurs
of the two women in the meadow grasses.
Envy the paper where everything is painted,
envy the invisible rose
that sets shadows on fire
and tousles neatly-combed hair.

# A meiga na esquina da barra

Amei naquela ollada
o que había de sospeita.
E o medo das cousas
tiña naquel espello a ilusión
de disentir do futuro.

# The Witch in the Corner of the Bar

What I loved about the look in her eye
was its air of suspicion.
And how the fear of things
reflected there harboured the hope
of defying the future.

# Vento tehuelche

Un par de orellas de tehuelche
valía unha libra esterlina.
Houbo cazadores de indios
que decidiron aforrar munición
e cobraron por orellas de vivo.
As ánimas que penduran nas pugas dos arames
das inmensas chacras
teñen esa desfigura inmortal.
Orientan o vento arfante
polo mudo territorio da morgue.
O laio intempestivo, incesante,
do único sobrevivente
á procura das matogueiras do ñire,
cunha raspa de perca nos dentes.
O vento,
o vento sen orellas,
o vento de ninguén,
bramando a verba infinda.

# Tehuelche Wind

A pair of Tehuelche ears
could fetch a pound sterling.
There were Indian-hunters
who decided to save ammunition
and cut them from the living.
The souls that hang from the barbed wire fences
around vast estates
have that same immortal mutilation.
They guide the panting wind
around the mute territory of the morgue.
The unseasonable, unceasing lament
of the sole survivor
in search of beech thickets
with a piece of cactus between his teeth.
The wind,
the earless wind,
wind of no-body
that howls the infinite word.

# Enterro campesiño

Só soaban as chocas
cunha alegría animal
pendurada das nubes,
abrindo ocos na herba,
no silencio abismal,
inhumano,
que ceibou a campá.

# Country Burial

The only sound was of cowbells
that hung from the clouds
with an animal cheerfulness,
opening spaces in the grass,
in the bottomless
inhuman silence
released by the church bell.

# Castro Laboreiro

Onde o baleirar da esfera
deixou esta beleza áspera.
Altares aleixoados
que apreixan os ceos.
Corpos abertos,
pedra esfolada
con emplastos de lique.
Esta beleza que fere e lambe:
Ou es de aquí
ou estás de máis.

# Castro Laboreiro

This is the place where the emptied sphere
left a rough beauty.
Amputated altars
that bite at the skies.
Opened bodies,
skinned stone
with lichen dressings.
This beauty that wounds and licks:
You are of this place
or you have no place here.

# Graffiti

Ti, quenquera que sexas, escoita nesta laxe a ánima que eu fun.
Un home feliz cando labrou a apocalipse no obradoiro de Mateo.
E os tres cabaliños da Adoración.
E a serea paxaro do magno coro, cun rostro que eu soñei
ao tempo que xurdía con mil e cento mil beixos do buril.
O cicel peiteou as súas longas guedellas.
Toda a vida sentín o abrazo das súas alas.
E catro pernas tiña.
De loba, de vaca brava.
Era quente por dentro como a pedra.

Ti, quenquera, se cadra non o sabes que a pedra é quente.
Como a montaña.
Os seus ollos son verdes. Escintilan no ocaso.
A pedra arde ás mans en lapa de azul noite.
Como a montaña, ten o sangue de baga, de vermello dragón.
Agradézolle á pedra ese amor que me deu.
A quentura, a compaña, no inferno dos meus días.

Ti, quenquera, se cadra non o sabes que a pedra fala.
Ela contou todo o que ves agora.
Venceu á morte, á paz eterna.
Aprendeume esta lingua que non leva o vento.

Ti, quenquera, eu fun amigo dela.
Non te deteña a culpa nin a piedade.
Leme en voz alta dende as entrañas.
Só quero oír da túa boca o que eu fun.

Ti, quenquera, eu fun amigo dela.
Canteiro en Compostela eu fun.
Eu fun o seu amigo, amigo dela.

# Graffiti

You, whoever you are, listen in this stone to the soul that I was.
A happy man when he carved the Apocalypse in Mateo's workshop.
And the three horses of the Adoration.
And the siren-bird of the *magno coro*, with a face I dreamed
into being with a thousand and ten thousand kisses of the burin.
The chisel combed her long hair.
My whole life I could feel the embrace of her wings.
Four legs she had.
Like a she-wolf, a stray cow.
She was hot inside, like stone.

You, whoever you are, perhaps you didn't know that stone is hot.
Like the mountain.
Its eyes are green. And turn gold at dusk.
Stone burns your hands with its blue night-flames.
Like the mountain it has berry blood, dragon-red.
I am grateful for the love it showed me.
The heat, the company, in the cold hell of my days.

You, whoever you are, perhaps you don't know that stone can speak.
It told me everything you can see here.
Defeated death and eternal peace.
Taught me a language the wind cannot blow away.

You, whoever you are, I was its friend.
Don't let shame or pity hold you back.
Read me out loud, from the heart.
I only want to hear who I was from your mouth.

You, whoever, I loved the stone.
Stone carver in Compostela.
A friend, a friend of stone.

# Metamorfose

Por moito que esculques,
quen ve é a noite,
a cámara escura do espello da terra.
Pecha os ollos. Escoita, Samsa.
Vai cara á primavera, ao violín,
ao incesto.

## Metamorphosis

For all your scrutiny
it's the night that sees,
camera obscura to the earth's mirror.
Close your eyes. Listen, Samsa.
And walk towards spring-time, violin-strings,
incest.

# Vangarda

Por que ves como un triunfo
que o vento
despece letra a letra
o letreiro luminoso da noite?
Que bárbaro, que estilo!

# Vanguard

Why do you see it as a victory
when the wind
dismantles, letter by letter,
the neon signs of the night?
So audacious, so full of style!

## Espiritual

No alto, no púlpito,
o crego interrógase sobre a forma
da terceira persoa,
do Espírito Santo.
E aboia no silencio de todos unha saudade.
A do toliño de Conxo
que movía as ás
rente do templo,
piando:
        —Son eu, son eu!

# Spiritual

On high, in the pulpit,
the priest ponders the form
of the third person,
the Holy Spirit.
And floating in the congregation's silence is a nostalgia.
A nostalgia for the madman of Conxo
who would flap his wings
from the church floor,
cheeping:
                "It's me, it's me".

# Resurrección

Levántate e anda!
Aí o Mesías estivo maxistral
e Lázaro non tivo máis remedio
que se render á ironía.
Resucitar, resucitar, resucitar?
Erguerse, andar.
Outra vez todo iso.
E ademais con publicidade.

# Resurrection

Arise and walk!
In that moment the Messiah was masterful
and Lazarus had no choice
but surrender to irony.
Come back? Come back to life?
Get up, walk.
Not all that again.
And this time the press were here.

# Terminus

Lembras? Non había nada
até que a natureza descubriu a exculpación.
Coa panca de óso do horizonte
ergueuse a primeira anta.
Miles de anos despois,
alí colocamos a botella
de vidro escuro verde,
alí, o disparo.
Ao redor da marca,
as cachizas escintilan ao sol,
lentes de cego
para ler o epitafio
do primeiro inmortal.

Eis a beleza bastarda do Canon.
O corpo devece o subtraído,
a materia informe dos cascallos,
o rescaldo do baleiro,
a preada insepulta.
Furtiva,
á procura de repostos,
a humanidade peregrina
ao depósito dos monstros.

# Terminus

Do you remember? There was nothing
until nature discovered exoneration.
The first menhir was raised
with the bone lever of the horizon.
Thousands of years later,
that's where we place the bottle
of dark green glass,
right there, the shot.
Around the mark it leaves
shards glitter in the sun,
a blind man's spectacles
to read the epitaph
of the first immortal.

This is the bastard beauty of the Canon.
The body desires all that was taken away,
the shapeless stuff of wreckage,
embers of the void,
unburied carrion.
Furtive,
in search of spare parts,
humanity makes its pilgrimage
to the warehouse of monsters.

# Historia do silencio

*A Francisco Javier Comesaña*

O corneta calou as cousas todas
e a noite ficou esperta,
elevada naquel silencio
que ía do aquén ao alén,
por riba das columnas
do bafo da intemperie
uniformada.

Dous, tres dedos cómicos,
rente do inverno,
entremetidos nas vísceras tráxicas
de astros
e recrutas.

Eu estiven alí e oíno.
Aquel silencio aquela noite.
Oín o calafrío,
aquela dor exquisita,
a beleza ferinte,
dunha maxestade sublevada.

«Moi ben ese toque, corneta»,
dixo o oficial de servizo.
Parco, engadiu: «Perfecto».
O intérprete do silencio respondeu:
«Se tivese outra boca, meu capitán,
aínda o faría mellor
o silencio».

Obtivo un permiso para baixar á cidade
e mercar o novo instrumental.
Endexamais volveu.

# A History of Silence

*For Francisco Javier Comesaña*

The bugle silenced every last thing
and woke up the night,
uplifted in the silence
that stretched from here to the beyond,
up above the vapour-columns
of uniformly
inclement elements.

Two, three comical fingers
at winter's edge,
reaching into the tragic innards
of stars
and conscripts.

I was there and I heard it.
That silence that very night.
I heard the shiver,
the exquisite pain,
the cutting beauty
of a majestic mutiny.

"Well sounded, bugler"
said the duty officer.
Adding brusquely, "Perfectly executed".
The interpreter of silence replied:
"If I had another mouth-piece, Captain,
I'd do even better. I'd play it to death."

He was granted leave to go into the city
and buy a new set of instruments.
He never came back.

O silencio, si. Pousa o seu voo
no ombreiro da noite
como unha desacougante amizade.

But the silence did. Perching
on the night's shoulder
like a dangerous friendship.

# Historia da arte

*A Antón Mouzo*

Estouno a ver o día máis fero,
despois do dioivo.
O río Pequeno saíu da toponimia,
rebordou canles e ribazos,
volveu a brañas e xunqueiras,
ás lagoas desecadas,
á memoria espoliada da auga.
A chea entrou no estudio do pintor
á procura das paisaxes,
de toda aquela materia esperta,
soñadora.
Alí estaba el, enfrontado á turba,
custodio de todas as vangardas,
volcánico, plutónico, anátido,
obsidiánico, astrográfico, ginkgófito,
anfibio.
Antón loitou contra o naufraxio,
salvou os cadros do afundimento.
E logo curounos un a un.
Os afogados, os enlamados, os fanados.
O seu estudio era un hospital de campaña.
Tiña unhas mans pequenas, lizgairas e sinceras,
de enfermeira de prematuros.
Quería que os seus cadros fosen felices.
Ou máis ben,
portadores dunha saudade desposuída
de tristura.
Talvez por iso o primeiro que reparou
foi as cordas dos violíns
da serie inconclusa das *Naturezas vivas,*
onde había tamén bidueiras, cabalos, garzas,

# A History of Art

*For Antón Mouzo*

I can still see him, that awful day
after the flood.
The river Pequeno had outgrown its toponymy,
burst its banks
and returned to reedbeds, meadows,
dry turloughs,
and the plundered memory of water.
The floodwaters invaded the painter's studio
in search of landscapes,
in search of all that waking,
dreaming matter.
And there he was, confronted by the crowding tumult,
custodian of all the vanguards,
volcanic, plutonic, anatidae,
obsidian, astrophotographic, ginkgophytic,
amphibious.
Antón fought against the flood,
rescued the paintings from the deep.
And brought them back to life one by one.
The drowned, the mud-smeared, the amputees.
The studio became a field hospital.
His hands were small, agile and earnest,
like a nurse who delivers premature babies.
He wanted his paintings to be happy.
Or rather,
to carry their longing
without sadness.
Perhaps for that reason the first things he repaired
were the violin strings
in an unfinished sequence of *Still Lifes*
that also included birch trees, horses, herons,

postes telefónicos, máquinas de coser,
e o par de botas do pai,
que andaba os camiños de lobo
para sandar electrodomésticos
e orientar as antenas
dos primeiros televisores.

telegraph posts, sewing machines,
the pair of boots belonging to his father,
who walked the paths of wolves
to heal domestic appliances
and tune the aerials
of the first television sets.

# Historia do diñeiro

O meu sombreiro, no chan da rúa, é o Banco de Europa.
Por favor, non guindedes tristura no meu pucho.
Non estou pedindo un par de ollos.
Non son un mendigo.
Escarvo no voso peto coa miña canción.
Canto como un mineiro galés en paro,
como o campesiño que pilla o derradeiro tren de Europa
á procura do carneiro de ás e vélaro dourado.
O meu sombreiro é o meu castelo, o meu país, o meu móbil.
Liberade as vosas mans!
Soltade as andoriñas!
Que as vosas moedas deixen ver a súa mitra.
Botade, polo menos, o custo dunha europea chamada perdida.
Teño que facer unha chamada telefónica á miña infancia.
Os nenos adoran o diñeiro.
Lembro o recendo a terra da miña primeira paga.
Axudamos a recoller as patacas.
O pai de Felipe deunos unha moeda da cor da prata,
un peso, cinco pesetas.
Tremelucía nas nosas sucias mans
mais nós mercamos cromos de deuses
ciclistas.
Outro día,
unha vella, Celia, a pescantina, chamou por min:
«Ei, rapaz! Vai á tenda e merca viño tinto
e unha bola de pan».
Fixen o choio de Xesús en Canaá.
A serea varada
deume unha moeda co recendo do mar.
Mais baixo as escamas,
atopei de novo a face do home feo,
Franco era o seu nome.

# A History of Money

My cap, on the ground, is the European Bank.
Please don't throw your sadness in it.
I'm not asking for your eyes.
I'm not a beggar.
I dig around in your pockets with my song,
sing like a Welsh miner on the dole,
like the farm labourer boarding the last train in Europe
in search of the winged ram and the golden fleece.
My cap is my castle, my homeland, my mobile phone.
Free up those hands!
Don't hedge your funds!
Show me the colour of your money.
Throw me, at least, the price of a missed call to Europe.
I need to make a phone-call to my childhood.
Children adore money.
I remember the earthy smell of my first pay.
We helped pick potatoes.
Felipe's father gave us a coin the colour of silver,
a peso, five pesetas.
It shone, glinting in our dirty hands,
but we bought picture cards of the gods
of cycling.
Another day,
Celia the old fish-woman, called to me:
"You, there! Go down to the shop and get me some red wine
and a loaf of bread."
I pulled a fast one like Jesus in Cana.
The beached siren
gave me a coin that smelled of the sea.
But beneath its scales
again I found the face of the ugly man.
His name was Franco.

Naquel tempo,
eu devecía por Cassius Clay.
Gustaríame cuñar moeda propia
co rostro do boxeador
ou a cara de Marisol,
a mociña que eu amaba
na escuridade do cinema.
Pobreza, pobreza é non ter un pouco de escuridade.
Unha vez, o meu avó díxome:
«Escoita! Leva sempre, sempre, diñeiro no teu peto.
O diñeiro é moi importante para a xente pobre.
Os ricos non levan pasta solta».
Contou a verdade.
El non era un euro-escéptico.
Era un mundo-escéptico,
mais gardaba un patacón de esperanza na súa boina.
Outra vez, fíxome esta irónica profecía:
«Non haberá Día do Xuízo Final. Mágoa!
Tiña eu interese polo peso das almas na romana de San Miguel.
Que pesará a alma? Un gran? Un ovo?
O tío Francisco dicía que un repolo, se é de home de ben».
O meu sombreiro, no chan, é un carrusel.
Coñezo o prezo do silencio.
O amargo espantoso prezo do silencio.
Por iso canto no recanto frío da rúa Europa.
Que pesará unha alma? Que pesará?
Lembro o mercurio dun termómetro roto,
os dedos enfebrecidos
á procura da partícula esférica.
Oía a manda dos cans pequenos,
a cadela do axóuxere,
o péndulo,
a luz estrondosa da lámpada.
Era imposíbel
devolver o fodido mercurio
ao interior do termómetro.

At that time
I worshipped Cassius Clay.
I would have liked to mint my own coinage
with the boxer's face on it,
or Marisol,
the girl I loved
in the darkness of the cinema.
Poverty, poverty is not having a little bit darkness.
Once, my grandfather told me:
"Listen! Always, always have money in your pocket.
Cash is very important for poor people.
The rich never carry loose change."
What he said was true.
He was no Euro-sceptic.
He was a World-sceptic,
but he kept his tuppence-worth of hope beneath his beret.
Another time, he foretold ironically:
"There won't be any Final Judgement Day. Pity!
I would have liked to know the weight of souls on St Michael's scales.
What does a soul weigh? Same as a grain of corn? An egg?
Your Uncle Francisco says an honest man's soul weighs as much
        as a cabbage."
My cap on the ground is a merry-go-round.
I know the price of silence.
The bitter, awful price of silence.
That's why I sing on this cold corner of Europe Street.
What does a soul weigh? How much?
I remember the mercury of a broken thermometer,
the fevered fingers
trying to find the silver ball.
I could hear the pack of small dogs,
the one with the bell,
the pulse of the pendulum,
the screaming light from the lamp.
It was impossible
to get the damned mercury
back inside the thermometer.

Cambiando de tema, ese mariñeiro
que ben capea o temporal.
Que ben leva o seu fardel de escuridade.
Que esvelto o seu segredo.

On a different subject,
see how that sailor weathers the storm.
Look how he carries his bundle of darkness.
How slender its secret.

# A man baleira (11-M)

Agora entendo
porque hai miles de anos
no cosmos do inverno
ti fuches cara ao fondo da cova
e pintaches a man baleira
co pigmento en chamas
da onomatopea máis xeada.

Así ficou
no ventre da custodia
a tatuaxe dos teus brazos amputados,
o beixo dos teus beizos esfolados.

Na man baleira
abriuse un corredor
ao eido do indelébel,
á nai dos ollos.

Aquela man
puxo fin á pintura dos bisontes,
ás escenas de caza,
á maxia,
ao sagrado, á decoración,
ao gabinete de curiosidades.
A túa man baleira era unha forma estraña.
Contíñao todo
e nela choraba, encrequenada, a nada.

# The Empty Hand (11-M)

Now I understand
why thousands of years ago
in winter's cosmos
you went to the very back of the cave
and painted an empty hand
with the flaming pigment
of the iciest onomatopoeia.

And so it stayed
in the custodian's womb,
the tattoo of your amputated eyes,
the kiss of your flayed lips.

In the empty hand
a passage opened
to the fields of the indelible,
to the origins of seeing.

That hand
put an end to the painting of bison
and hunting scenes,
to magic,
the sacred, to decoration
and the curiosity cabinet.
Your empty hand had a strange anatomy.
It contained everything,
and in it, crouched and crying, was nothing.

# Vieira Pop-Art

*A XGG*

O croar,
o grallar,
o bruar,
o chiar,
o laiar das cores espoliadas
nos salóns decorativos.
As cores escravas fan buracos no teito:
un derrube de anxos
e bagas azuis de folerpas estampadas no abraio
de quen foi aquén
nalgures.
As tampas dos ollos
abren o sartego da historia:
unha vieira á altura do corazón
abandonada por un home en armas
no paraíso belicoso do ceo.
Velaí á fin a historia:
pop-art
e menos mal.

# Scallop Pop-Art

*For XGG*

The croaking,
the cawing,
the screeching,
the squawking,
the lamentations of plundered colours
in ornate salons.
Enslaved colours make holes in the ceiling:
angels come tumbling down
with blue berries trampled in the panic
of someone who was here,
somewhere.
Eyelids
open the sepulchre of history:
a scallop-shell worn next to the heart
abandoned by an armed man
in the warring paradise of heaven.
Here at last is history:
pop-art,
and just as well.

# O Canon

Eu, non o Doríforo, era o verdadeiro Canon,
a medida perfecta,
que un día naceu no obradoiro de Polícleto.
Apreixado polos ladróns de arte,
despois de infernal viaxe,
cheguei a Roma
onde conseguín fuxir nun descoido dos raptores.
Caín rodando por unha escada.
Escachei, pois.
Deixei polos chanzos
a dor áurea,
o desacougo xeométrico,
a preada da pedra.
E Pasquino, a estatua impertinente,
proclamou:
Velaí a medida perfecta.
Sen máis:
unha bela cabeza que perdeu a guerra.

# The Canon

I, not the Spear-Bearer, was the true Canon,
perfectly proportioned,
who came to life one day in Polykleitos' studio.
Taken prisoner by art-thieves,
after a hellish journey
I arrived in Rome,
where I caught my captors off guard and escaped.
I rolled all the way down a staircase.
Of course I was shattered.
I left behind me on the steps
golden pain,
geometric dread,
butchered stone.
And Pasquino, that upstart statue,
declared:
So much for perfect proportion.
There you have it:
a beautiful head that lost the war.

# Tons de gris baixo o ceo

En Tinduf,
nun curral feito con chatarra bélica,
primeiro e último circo do universo,
xeometría caída
a piques de despegar cara á heliopausa.
En Tinduf,
no escouredo do éxodo,
nun curral arqueolóxico,
ruínas do futuro,
cascallos gris cinza de materia interestelar,
a fauna do choque de terminación,
unha cabra con ollos de gris lobo
á que só interesa a información básica,
natural, da miña sombra
impresa na saudade do papel,
esa cabra da galaxia Gutenberg
devece polas follas do meu xornal,
roe con pracer apocalíptico a primeira páxina,
os grandes titulares resultan sabedeiros,
segue coa súa boca
unha orde tipográfica,
unha axenda de corrosión global,
avanza pola sección de inmóbeis gris platino,
devora gris toldo con vistas ao mar,
hectáreas hipotecadas de gris mofo,
degusta a vangarda publicitaria,
a sinestesia pop,
o verdor automobilístico,
o shocking pink do plástico carnal,
o gris turbio, excitante, dos sucesos,
e agora trisca
os obituarios ilustres,

# Shades of Grey under the Sun

In Tinduf,
in a yard made of wartime scrap,
first and last circle of the Universe,
fallen geometry
about to lift off for the heliopause.
In Tinduf,
on the stony ground of exodus,
in an archeological site
lie ruins of the future,
ash-grey debris of interstellar stuff,
the fauna of the final crash,
a goat with wolf-grey eyes
interested only in the fundamentals,
naturally, of my shadow
printed on the exile of paper,
this goat from the Gutenberg galaxy
craves the pages of my newspaper,
swallows with apocalyptic pleasure the front page,
savours the flavour of the headlines,
systematically chomping
through typographic order,
a diary of global corrosion;
advancing through the platinum grey Property Section,
it devours grey awnings with sea views,
mould-grey mortgaged hectares,
relishing the latest big thing in advertising,
pop synaesthesia,
racing-green,
the shocking pink of plastic flesh,
the troubling, provocative grey of the news,
and now, sinks its teeth
into illustrious obituaries,

ese gris cadavérico,
a pálida cultura,
o festín.

that cadaverous grey,
pallid culture,
the banquet.

# Unha chamada perdida

Aí está, es ti, nun ring interior.
*Repito posición:*
*Golf Alfa Lima India Charlie India Alfa*
Aínda que creo que ti,
precisamente ti, quen o diría,
tes algo de esperanza.
Hai nos teus ollos un letreiro de neon.
O neon pertence á vangarda da esperanza.
Lembras?
*A mensaxe era:*
*Lima India Bravo Echo Romeo Delta Alfa Delta Echo*
As fotografías apreixaban o jazz da luz.
Os amantes abaneaban
no acordeón do *L'Atalante*.
O neon brillaba
coa memoria dun río
no traxe branco de Dita Parlo.
Os beixos eran longos,
duraban máis que a fin.
Por eles perdíanse os tranvías
e os barcos.
*Como era a mensaxe?*
*Alfa Mike Oscar Romeo*
*Outra vez:*
*Alfa Mike Oscar Romeo*
E os pais desacougados vomitaban a factura eléctrica,
boxeadores sen bisté nos corredores da noite noite.
Dende entón,
noto que tes algo de esperanza,
unha araña bébeda de trebón
que prende nas espiñas das nubes de abril,
un lixo de arco iris no ollo

# Missed Call

There you are, it's you, sparring again.
*Repeat position:*
*Golf Alpha Lima India Charlie India Apha*
Though I believe that you,
yes, you, (who would have thought it?)
still harbour some hope.
There are neon signs in your eyes
and neon is the light of hope's vanguard.
Remember?
*The message was:*
*Foxtrot Romeo Echo Echo Delta Oscar Mike*
The photographs captured the light's jazz.
Lovers swayed
to the accordion of *L'Atalante*.
Neon lights glittered
with the memory of a river
in Dita Parlo's white suit.
Kisses were long,
they went on long after the end.
Trains and boats were missed
on their account.
*How did that message go?*
*Lima Oscar Victor Echo*
*And again:*
*Lima Oscar Victor Echo*
Distraught parents threw up the electricity bill,
steakless boxers in the corridors of the deadest night.
Since then,
I've noticed you still harbour some hope,
a drunk spider in the storm
that clings to wisps of April clouds,
a speck of rainbow in the eye

como os pescadores de Fisterra,
un peixe boca de fogo,
un peixe que cría as ovas entre os dentes.
*Repito posición:*
*no ring interior,*
*emitindo para un sistema exterior.*
*Cal é a mensaxe? Cambio.*
*Cal é a mensaxe?*

like the fishermen of Finisterre,
a firemouth,
a fish that carries its eggs between its teeth.
*Repeat position:*
*In the ring with yourself,*
*shadowboxing with the world.*
*What is your message? Over.*
*What is your message?*

# Boh

Era dun andar lento,
pensativos pés escrutadores
dun home sorprendido de estar vivo.
A derradeira obra foi a máquina asombrosa,
un carro do país
estraño aos nosos ollos como unha aeronave
medieval
que el construíu nun furancho urbano.
Era o tempo de ir á lúa,
de pisala, ferrala,
mais el mediu o transporte
para traela ao val
polas rutas do esterco e mais das algas.
Dicía: Boh, boh, boh, boh!

Tamén facía esquinas,
xusto o ángulo que necesita un home
para que non lle dispare a Historia polas costas.
Abriu co gume do seu corpo
un recanto na taberna.
Respectábase o lugar porque o fixera el,
cara a dentro,
tallando a sombra
cun machado de silencio.
Fixera a luz da lámpada
cos filamentos do seu cabelo crecho,
un branco de cinc incendiado de paz
atormentada.
Dicía: Boh, boh, boh, boh!

Facía coas mans cada cigarro
e o fume leal,

# Boh

He was a slow-walking man,
with the thoughtful, searching feet
of one surprised to be alive.
The last thing he made was his wonder-craft,
a country cart
as alien to our eyes as a medieval
airship
which he built in an urban hovel.
It was the age of flying to the moon
so men could leave their mark on it,
but he fine-tuned transportation
that would carry it
down pathways of seaweed and manure
saying: Boh, boh, boh, boh!

He also built corners
at the precise angle a man needs
so History won't shoot him in the back.
Used the side of his body
to mark out a corner in the bar.
A place respected because he had made it,
turning inwards,
cleaving shadow
with an axe of silence.
He also made the lamplight
with filaments of his curling hair,
white as scorched zinc -
the colour of peace in torment,
saying: Boh, boh, boh, boh!

His hands crafted every cigarette
and its loyal smoke,

pesaroso,
era o cordal
que sostiña un descoñecido país
enriba das nubes.
Un infindo centeal
enxertado
nos últimos paxaros.
Dicía: Boh, boh, boh, boh!

Dentro da noite,
unha noite ao pasar,
a voz sacerdotal:
«Faille falta un responso, Manuel!».
E el subiu ao alto
de si mesmo,
a derradeira voz
na derradeira estada: Boh!

Amei aquela música,
o gorgolexar da soidade,
os dedos sinceros a apañar
os dentes do leite que morderon o xeo,
os ósos miúdos do son tumefacto,
os borboriños que abrollaban do chan,
o scat dun jazzman,
dicía: Boh, boh, boh, boh!

Nunca nada pediu o carpinteiro.
Todo o fixo el
coas mans.
Mesmo a sombra para andar
o día de marchar.
Dicía: Boh, boh, boh, boh!

rising dolefully,
was the mountain range
that held an unknown country
up above the clouds.
An endless rye-field
grafted
onto the highest-flying birds,
saying: Boh, boh, boh, boh!

Within the night
a darker night,
and the priest's voice:
*Pray for the repose of the souls, Manuel!*
And he climbed up to the highest point
of himself,
to the highest voice
on the highest scaffolding: Boh!

I loved to hear that music,
the gurgling song of solitude,
honest fingers
picking up the milk teeth that had bitten into ice,
small bones of swollen sound,
mutterings that sprouted from the ground,
a jazzman's scat,
saying: Boh, boh, boh, boh!

The carpenter never asked for anything,
he made everything
with his own hands.
Even a shadow to walk
the day of the last march,
saying: Boh, boh, boh, boh!

# Mayday

*Mayday, mayday, mayday!*
*Pan-pan, pan-pan, pan-pan!*
*Securité, securité, securité!*

Alarma. Aviso de Auxilio.
Noroeste cuarta Oeste.
Asañado o silencio de si mesmo,
toda a frota está á escoita,
toda a frota está á espreita.

Os reloxos penduran aforcados
nos traxes de loito.
Os cabalos de pedra
corren cara ao mar.
Nos secadoiros do congro
abanean pelellos de vento.
O sol lambe as feridas do solpor.
O sol crava os ollos con noxo
no coágulo da súa sombra granate.
A derradeira lavandeira
descompón as seis cores
e o anil
no prisma da súa man,
no lombo gris do río.
As máquinas de coser
foxen polos tellados,
fan zurcido invisíbel
co bafo dos ausentes.
A lúa é unha candea
na cabaza do medo.
O medo na redoma das mans.

# Mayday

*Mayday, mayday, mayday!*
*Pan-pan, pan-pan, pan-pan!*
*Securité, securité, securité.*

Siren. Distress call.
North-West quartering West.
Shamed silence,
the entire fleet is listening in,
the entire fleet on the alert.

Pocket-watches dangle like hanged men
from mourning-suits.
Stone horses
bolt towards the sea.
In the drying sheds
eel-skins swing in the wind.
The sun licks the dusk's wounds.
The sun fixes its bored gaze
on its clotted, crimson shadow.
The last washerwoman
separates the six colours
plus the indigo
in the prism of her hand,
on the river's grey back.
Sewing machines
flee across rooftops,
making invisible repairs
with the breath of the dead.
The moon is a candle
in fear's pumpkin-head.
Fear held in cupped hands.

*Mayday, mayday, mayday!*
*Pan-pan, pan-pan, pan-pan!*
*Securité, securité, securité!*

Medo meu,
meu irmán,
can do fusco
a trousar as cores do baleiro,
os ósos de Deus,
na esquina con gume de navalla.
Nubes dos cen mil estorniños da Coruña,
vou desfacer convosco,
cantou Pucho Boedo,
ese nó que nos ata.
Vou poñer na botoeira,
como flor degolada,
a bala que nos mata.

*Mayday, mayday, mayday!*
*Pan-pan, pan-pan, pan-pan!*
*Securité, securité, securité!*

Hai un cetáceo metrallado na Zambela,
a carón do Portiño.
Duro é de roer o óso da saudade.
Vou limar unha chave co óso da saudade,
a agulla do vinilo,
os dous dedos que Django salvou do inferno
das flores de plástico.
Os invernos tiñan tanta fame tanta
que rilaban as raíces das lámpadas,
as brasas que pisaban os faquires,
as bandadas de pésames,
o acento dos gonzos,
o dorso do abrente na moreira.
E logo o entebrecer,
o rudimento de non ser.

*Mayday, mayday, mayday!*
*Pan-pan, pan-pan, pan-pan!*
*Securité, securité, securité!*

This fear is mine,
old childhood companion,
the twilight dog
that vomits the colours of the void,
God-bones,
on knife-edged corners.
Clouds of Corunna's hundred thousand starlings,
I'm going to untie, with your help,
sang Pucho Boedo,
the knot that binds us.
And in my buttonhole,
like a decapitated flower,
I'll wear the bullet that kills us.

*Mayday, mayday, mayday!*
*Pan-pan, pan-pan, pan-pan!*
*Securité, securité, securité.*

A whale, machine-gunned on Zambela Island,
right beside O Portiño.
The bone of exile is hard to gnaw.
I'm going to file a key with the bone of homesickness,
the needle in the vinyl grooves,
the two fingers Django saved from the inferno
of burning plastic flowers.
The winters were so hungry, so hungry
they gnawed at the roots of lamps,
the hot coals walked by fakirs,
the flocks of condolences,
the squeaking of hinges,
the far side of dawn in the mulberry tree.
And then the darkening,
first principle of non-being.

O lugar máis quente era o billete de embarque,
aquela begonia no escaparate
cos teus ollos de óxido.
Ou un colchón de lá
        se ti a carón
        acaroados
aboiando
nese tremente adeus
que nos retivo unidos.

*Mayday, mayday, mayday!*
*Pan-pan, pan-pan, pan-pan!*
*Securité, securité, securité!*

The hottest place was a boarding-pass,
that shop-window begonia
with your rust-red eyes.
Or a wool mattress
   holding you fast
   two boats rafted
afloat
on that tremulous parting
that kept us together.

*Mayday, mayday, mayday!*
*Pan-pan, pan-pan, pan-pan!*
*Securité, securité, securité.*

# O subtraccionismo

Engadir á relación de efectos subtraídos:

O corpo do Canon verdadeiro,
a cabeza de Nike, a que desata a sandalia,
o pene do sátiro en repouso de Praxiteles,
o touro que, en 1631, Felipe IV matou cun tiro de arcabuz,
un ollo de Camões,
a vaixela do *Nautilus,*
un brazo de Valle-Inclán,
o pelo pubiano da muller espida nun diván vermello
que pintou Modigliani,
a verdade da morte de Eugeni Bonaventura de Vigo i Sallés,
a Walther 9 mm. do capitán Líster e a pluma de Machado,
o maletín de Walter Benjamin,
o xersei de la vermella do prisioneiro Gurkanov en Kolimá,
os dentes da infancia de Ángel González,
a espiga que medraba na man de Maruxa Mallo,
os metros de *Touch of Evil* de Orson Welles,
a auga do río Xallas na fervenza do Ézaro,
a voz de Miguelón xusto antes do cásting para *Os Miserábeis,*
aquel lugar, aquela casa. Aqueles ollos nos codelos das cancións.
A cicatriz da fiestra que cortaba en diagonal o ceo.
A simetría incandescente da pel do frío.
As cores mariñeiras daquel lume.
A neve da cámara de Herbert Ponting, despois da expedición de Scott
á Antártida.
O día de descanso.

# Taking Stock

To be added to the sum of missing stock:

The body of the original Canon,
the head of Nike, who unfastens her sandal,
the penis of Praxiteles' Leaning Satyr,
a bull killed in 1631 by Philip IV with an harquebus,
one of Camões' eyes,
crockery from the *Nautilus*,
Valle-Inclán's missing arm,
the pubic hair of the nude on a red divan
painted by Modigliani,
the truth about the death of Eugeni Bonaventura de Vigo i Sallés,
Captain Líster's 9mm Walther and Antonio Machado's pen,
Walter Benjamin's briefcase,
the red woollen sweater worn by prisoner Gurkanov in Kolyma,
the children's missing teeth in Ángel González's poem,
the ears of corn sprouting from Maruja Mallo's fingers,
the clips cut from Orson Welles' *Touch of Evil,*
water from the river Xallas in the Ézaro falls,
Miguelón's voice just before auditioning for *Les Misérables,*
that place, that house. Those eyes in the scraps of songs.
The sky, scarred by the window's oblique angle.
The cold's skin, its burning symmetry.
The colours of the sea in those flames.
The snow in Herbert Ponting's camera after Scott's expedition
to the Antarctic.
The day of rest.

# Así se fai un poeta

*A Avilés de Taramancos*

Mesmo a auga era muda.
Un aeroplano sulfatou os pentagramas
e o pesticida matou os pronomes persoais.
Os homes falaban con bocados de fume
e onomatopeas de banda deseñada
con moitas caídas
polo oco da néboa,
chisssst, plaf, catacroc, tumba.
Había mulleres que pronunciaban cores,
triángulos marelos,
círculos azuis
e cadrados negros.
Os beizos eran dúas lachas
de pedra das ánimas.
O neno durmía cunha buguina
debaixo da almofada.
E Lela da Pastora
díxolle de ollos en verdes labaradas:
      —Ti, rapaz, sempre a facer torres no ar!

# How to Make a Poet

*For Avilés de Taramancos*

Even the water was speechless.
A plane dusted the stars
and the pesticide killed all the personal pronouns.
Men spoke in mouthfuls of smoke
and comic-book onomatopoeias
with lots of falling
through gaps in the fog,
wheeee, splat, crash, ka-boom.
There were women who spoke in colours,
yellow triangles,
blue circles
and black squares.
Their lips, two chips
off the old block of souls.
The boy slept with a conch
beneath his pillow.
And Lela da Pastora,
with green flames in her eyes, said:
  "Don't ever give up building castles in the air".

# O valor das cousas

Arrastraba a pesadume de crer
que nada merecía ser furtado.
Leu no xornal
que andaban a roubar os santos,
os cruceiros,
e as campás das igrexas.
Ese sino
devolveulle algo de fe na humanidade:
o son dunha antiga arela
que o abranguía todo.

# The Value of Things

He used to drag around the weighty belief
that nothing deserved to be stolen.
Then he read in the paper
they were robbing holy statues,
stone crosses,
and even church bells.
That sign
gave him back some faith in human nature:
the sound of an ancient longing
that touched everything.

# Alalá
*Á vella maneira*

*A Cachi e Amparo*

Eu de noite iría de noite,
no medio do temporal.
Ir de día á luz do día
dáme medo, miña nai.

No fondo do teu ollare
unha gamela abanea.
Quen se puidera afogare
na ardora dunha misteira.

O que soño é verdade
como o silencio é un falare.
Se roubei o teu retrato
foi pra aprender a mirare.

Eu non sabía que había
tanta alegría nas bágoas
nin neve nas bidueiras
nin esperanza nas mágoas.

# Alalá
*In the old style*

*For Cachi and Amparo*

At night, at night, I would go at night,
in the middle of a storm.
To go by day, by the light of day
would cause me great alarm.

In the depths of your fathomless eyes
there rocks a little skiff.
And happy is the man who drowns
in the sea your love has lit.

All that I dream is the simple truth,
like silence, a kind of speech.
I only stole your picture
so I could learn to see.

I did not know that there could be
such joy in the midst of woe,
nor snow atop the birch trees
nor hope in all my sorrow.

## Guia práctica

E ti, tamén,
entre as maceiras,
sexas benvida
Raíña Branca do Canadá,
á par da Raíña das Reinetas.
Saúde e Terra,
Granny Smith.
Salve, Elstar.
Aló vén o Jerseymac
coa Verde Doncela.
Starking Delicious:
Fico aos teus pés.
Agarda a gravidade
cun anhelo escarlata.
Sexa tamén benvido
o Bo Cristián de Williams,
o galán das pereiras.
Convosco vou,
Raíña Claudia D'Ouillins
e Mirabella de Nancy,
a das pencas vermellas.
Cante o merlo,
saciado de cereixa,
unha cantiga púrpura
en brazos da Noire de Schneider.
Eu perdín
aquela que chamaban A Beleza,
a mazá máis roubada nas hortas da Galiza.
Só queda o verme do esplendor:
A lembranza dun riso prohibido.

# A Practical Guide

And you, too,
are most welcome
amongst apple trees,
Canadian Queen,
rival of the King of Pippins.
Health and Home be yours
Granny Smith.
All hail, Elstar.
Here comes Jerseymac
with a Green Lady.
Starking Delicious:
I kneel at your feet.
Gravity waits
with scarlet desire.
And you too are most welcome
William, Bon Chrétien,
Adonis of pear trees.
With you ladies I will go anywhere,
Claudia D'Oullins, queen of plums
and Mirabelle of Nancy
with your russet freckles.
Let the blackbird sing
a purple-hued song,
sated by cherries
in the arms of a Noire de Schneider.
I lost
the one they called Bonnie Best,
most robbed apple from the orchards of Galicia.
All that's left is the worm in glory's apple:
the memory of forbidden laughter.

## Toque de oración

O que máis xuraba era quen máis cría.
Lembro o aceno daquel mendigo,
disparando torta
a piadosa maldición.
Se as pedras falasen,
como Lucas quería,
terían esa mesma precisión.
Pelexaba con Deus,
ao xeito dun sparring
contra o Gran Campión.
Á terceira palabra
escachizou o ceo
e un lixo de lusco-fusco
cegoulle a visión.
Para el foi a moeda de miña nai
e o cicel da lembranza.
Tamén eu hei probar,
alzar
cara ao máis alto
as palmas e a queixada:
Deteña esta guerra,
ordénollo, Señor!

Escribín xa unha carta ao xornal,
vinte liñas de suco ben domado,
onde omitín o que máis me importaba:
Chegará o 18 de maio a Reykiavik
a andoriña exipcia
como todos os anos e hai xa miles?
Tamén asinei un manifesto
dirixido ao presidente.
En termos sensatos,

# Call to Prayer

The biggest blasphemer believed the most.
I remember the beggar's sneer
as he took a crooked aim
and fired his pious curse.
If stones could talk,
as Luke would have it,
they'd be just as accurate.
He fought with God
the way a sparring partner fights
against the Champ.
By the third word
he'd left the heavens in bits
and a splinter of twilight
had blinded his vision.
For him alone my mother's coin
and the chisel of memory.
I also have to try,
raise
as high as I can
my palms, my chin:
Stop this war,
I command you, Lord!

I already wrote a letter to the newspaper,
twenty lines of well-trodden terrain,
where I omitted the thing that mattered to me most:
Will the swallow from Egypt arrive
on May 18 in Reykjavik
like every other year and thousands past?
I also signed a manifesto
addressed to the President.
In reasonable,

é dicir, lamentábeis.
Invoquei a paz con moira xente
e sentín nos beizos as cóxegas de terra
desta palabra que lisca entre flores
como unha rata do camposanto.
A miña derradeira esperanza é vostede, Señor,
Deus Pai Taciturno.
Vexo que o presidente o trata con moita confianza.
Mesmo din que vostede está no allo,
que é Il Capo dei capi, o Don, o Mero mero.
Permítame que garde as distancias.
Eu non comparto esa camaradaxe.
Só conservo un electrón de fe,
é dicir, o chisco invisíbel,
a vergoña.
Por razóns de publicidade,
permítame que o maldiga dende o máis baixo,
abaneando na rúa da Merda,
tamén chamada Verea do Polvorín,
afogada a miña alma nun tetrabrik de viño Don Simón,
mentres Isaías,
bo e pelma,
me predica dende a outra beira:
«Como é que caíches así,
luz da mañá?».

No nome da culpa,
no nome do pecado,
no nome do pegañento medo
que carena os meus ósos,
esíxolle, Señor, que deteña esta guerra,
ordénollo, Señor.

which is to say, deplorable terms.
With many others I called for peace
and felt on my lips the earthy tingle
of that word that slinks off into the flowers
like a graveyard rat.
You are my last remaining hope, Lord.
God the Taciturn Father.
I see the President confides in you.
They say you're in the know,
that you're the capo dei capi, the Don, the big fish.
I'm not a part of your clique.
All I have left is one electron of faith,
the invisible particle known as
shame.
To get some publicity
allow me to curse you from the gutter,
staggering down Shit Street,
also known as Powder Keg Path,
my soul drowned in a carton of Don Simón wine,
while Isaiah,
that virtuous bore,
preaches from the other side of the street:
"How art thou fallen so low,
star of the morning?"

In the name of guilt,
in the name of sin,
in the name of the viscous fear
that coats my bones
I demand, Lord, that you stop this war.
I command it, Oh Lord.

# Terra de Fogo

Os turistas espreguízanse e excítanse
cando a crista do glaciar escacha.
Ese derrubamento da natureza gótica
provoca exclamacións de xubiloso abraio.
Talvez retrocede por vergoña,
talvez polos disparos dos flaxes,
talvez polos laios de asombro.
O éxito, a extinción.
A natureza, si, imita a arte.

# Tierra del Fuego

Tourists rouse and come to life
when the crest of the glacier cracks open.
The collapse of its natural gothic
raises shouts of horrified delight.
Perhaps it retreats out of shame,
perhaps it flees the flashing cameras,
the thrill-seekers' shouts.
Success, extinction.
Nature imitates art.

## Ósos e tellas

Bebe, pardal, as nubes
no púcaro das calas.
Deixa, Señor,
que goberne a miña soidade.
Árbores das estradas,
sicómoros,
pasade de man a man
este fardel de culpa,
os ósos das palabras,
deica chegar
á sección dos badalos,
á fundición soterrada do sino.
Permite, Señor,
que sinta o calafrío
desoutro metal,
a chave do desterro.
Bebe, pardal, as nubes
no púcaro onde a nada
constrúe a simetría
boca abaixo.
Concédeme, Señor,
unha libra de sal
para salgar o medo
que atesouro.
Deixa que goberne a miña soidade.
E oco a oco,
retellar o destino.

# Bones and Roof-Tiles

Drink up the clouds, little sparrow,
from the bowls of calla lilies.
Permit me, Oh Lord,
to govern my solitude.
Trees by the roadside,
sycamores,
pass from hand to hand
this bundle of guilt,
the bones of words,
till they come
to the place where bell-clappers are forged,
the subterranean casting of bells.
Permit me, Oh Lord,
to feel the frisson
of that other metal,
the key to exile.
Drink up the clouds, little sparrow,
from the bowl where emptiness
shapes symmetry
upside down.
Grant me, Oh Lord,
a pound of salt
to season this fear
that I hoard.
Let me govern my solitude.
And breach by breach,
repair the roof of fate.

# O corvo de Noé

A pomba cumpriu a misión.
         Volveu á arca
e deitou o signo na man de Noé.
Mais o corvo afastouse
nun refacho de vento,
saíu da historia
do escarmento divino
cun trazo desastrado,
pintou con ás o autorretrato
do voar farrapento,
signo el mesmo
do lévedo inmortal do despoxo,
e foi pousar na identidade prófuga da neve.
Todo está nesa voz
leal á soidade.
Gralla con humor negro o desertor.
Parodia o estilo marcial de Deus.
Roucas voces de mando,
e unha piadosa maldición enxertada no vento,
esa lápida nómade
que de todo home debería dicir:
         *Morreu porque el quixo*

# Noah's Raven

The dove completed its mission.
        Returned to the ark
and dropped the sign into Noah's hand.
But the raven flew off
in a gust of wind,
quit the story
of the divine lesson
with an untidy flourish,
painted with its wings a self-portrait
of ragged flight,
itself a sign
of the immortal ferment of loss,
then came to rest on the fugitive identity of snow.
Everything is in that voice
so loyal to solitude.
It caws with the deserter's black humour.
Parodies God's martial tones.
Hoarse shouts of command,
and a pious curse chiselled onto the wind,
that itinerant headstone
that should say of every man:
        *He died because he chose to.*

# Notes / Glossary

### The Enigmatic Order (p.15)
Marcos Valcárcel López (1958–2010) was a Galician historian, journalist and writer.

### Cantiga de amor (p.29)
The 1680 *cantigas* (songs), were written in Galician-Portuguese between the 12th and 14th centuries. They can be divided into three basic genres: male-voiced love poetry, called *cantigas de amor*, female-voiced love poetry, called *cantigas de amigo*; and poetry of insult and mockery called *cantigas d'escarnho e de mal dizer*. The language they were written in can be sourced to the vernacular spoken north and south of the Minho River (which divides Galicia from Portugal). This was the preferred language of lyric poets from all over the Iberian peninsula at this time, with the exception of Catalonia. The songs were collected in *cancioneiros* (song books) and rediscovered in the 18th and 19th centuries.

### Lighthouse Hill (p.31)
The title alludes to the location of Hercules' Lighthouse in the poet's native city of A Coruña (Corunna), in the area of the city known as *Monte Alto*. The lighthouse was built in the first century AD and is said to be the oldest working lighthouse in the world.

According to Indian legend, a jealous tyrant of Kashmir sought to murder a handsome young man, but when passing through a market was stopped in his tracks by the mocking laughter of a fish on one of the stalls. He realised the folly of his vanity and the young man's life was spared.

### The Homecoming (p.35)
Luis Ángel Sánchez Pereiro, aka Lois Pereiro (1958–1996) was a Galician poet and writer. In 2011, the annual *Galician Literature Day* was dedicated to him. His *Collected Poems* are published in English.

### Waiting for Ángel González (p.45)
The term Edda is from the Old Norse and alludes to the *Poetic Edda* and *Prose Edda*, both of which were written down in Icelandic during

the 13th century. The *Poetic Edda*, also known as the *Elder Edda*, is a collection of 34 Old Norse poems from the Icelandic medieval manuscript, the *Codex Regius*.

### Castro Laboreiro (p.55)
The title alludes to a place in the North of Portugal, in the region of Tras-Os-Montes.

### Graffiti (p.57)
Master Mateo (active 1168–1188) is the name given to the anonymous Romanesque sculptor whose greatest work is the triple doorway in the Cathedral of Santiago de Compostela, known as the *Pórtico da Gloria*.

### Terminus (p.67)
An architectural term for a figure of a human bust or animal ending in a square pillar from which it appears to spring; originally a boundary marker in ancient Rome.

### A History of Silence (p.69)
Francisco Javier Comesaña (1962–2011) was a classical violinist. Son of republican exiles in Mexico, he studied music in Mexico and Russia. Between 1974 and 2003 he worked with the Symphonic Orchestra of Radiotelevisión Española.

### A History of Art (p.73)
Antón Mouzo Lavandeira was a Galician painter. He was born in Vimianzo, in the province of A Coruña, in 1957, and died in 2007.

### A History of Money (p.77)
The dog with the bell is a part of Galician folklore, an animal who sometimes accompanies the *Santa Compaña*, the procession of the dead.

### The Empty Hand (p.83)
11-M is the journalistic abbreviation used in Spain for the al-Qaeda attack on the commuter rail system on March 11, 2004, that killed 191 people and wounded 1,800.

## Scallop Pop-Art (p.85)
The identity of XGG is Xesús González Gómez, a critic who has published extensively on vanguard movements in both literature and the visual arts.

## Missed Call (p.93)
Dita Parlo (1906–1971) was a German actress. Her first film appearance was in *Homecoming* in 1928. During the 1930s she appeared in both German and French language films, achieving success in such films as *L'Atalante* (1934) and *La Grande Illusion* (1937). *L'Atalante* was directed by Jean Vigo, the son of Eugeni Bonaventura de Vigo i Sallés.

## Mayday (p.101)
José "Pucho" Boedo (1928–1986) was a singer who acquired mythical status in his native Galicia. He was a member of the group *Los Tamara*, sang with Alfonso Saavedra's Band *Los Trovadores,* and went on to perform with *Los Satélites* and many other artists in Spain and Latin America.

At the age of 18, Django Reinhardt was injured in a fire. To supplement their income his wife made artificial flowers out of celluloid, a highly flammable material. One night he knocked over a candle and started a fire in their caravan. He was quickly pulled to safety, but received first- and second-degree burns over half his body. His right leg was paralysed and the third and fourth fingers of his left hand were badly burned. With rehabilitation and practice he adapted to playing in a new way, and played all of his guitar solos with only two fingers.

## Taking Stock (p.107)
The iconoclastic Galician novelist, playwright and poet Ramón María del Valle Inclán (1866–1936), was born in Vilanova de Arousa. In 1899, as a result of a brawl with fellow-writer Manuel Bueno, he lost his left arm.

Eugeni Bonaventura de Vigo i Sallés (aka Miguel Almereyda, 1883–1917), was a militant Catalonian anarchist and founder and editor of the French radical journal *La Guerre Sociale*. He made many enemies among the French Government during World War I. In August 1917 he was arrested on a charge of treason and, a week later, was found dead in his cell in suspicious circumstances.

Ángel González (1925–2008), was one of a generation of Spanish poets known as the 'Generación del 50'. The poem alluded to is 'Menos mal que todavía me queda el esqueleto' ('At least I still have my skeleton') where the poet laments all the teeth lost by Spanish children due to post-war malnutrition, and wonders where they may have gone.

Avant-garde painter Maruja Mallo (1902–1995) was born in the Galician province of Lugo. The image in the poem alludes to some of her Surrealist works, such as *Sorpresa del trigo* (1936) and *El canto de la espiga* (1939).

Miguelón (Miguel Ladrón de Guevara). A young, Galician singer with dance-bands from the Labañou district of Corunna. He lost his voice while performing one night, just before he was due to take a final audition for a leading role in the musical, *Les Misérables*, in Madrid.

How to Make a Poet (p.109)
Avilés (1935–1992) was born in the village of Taramancos (hence his literary name), very near Noia, in the province of Corunna. His real name was Antón Avilés Vinagre. Lela da Pastora was his mother, and her comment in the poem is the opening epigraph of one of his best-known poetry collections, the title of which is also taken from the same comment: *As torres no ar* (1989).

Alalá (p.113)
The *alalá* has been described as the oldest and most characteristic form of Galician traditional music. It has survived thanks to popular, oral tradition, and many examples were collected and transcribed by poets and musicians of the Romantic era. The origin of the *alalá* form, and its relationship with other musical forms, particularly religious, have attracted many and varied theories by musicologists.

www.ingramcontent.com/pod-product-compliance
Lightning Source LLC
Chambersburg PA
CBHW031152160426
43193CB00008B/342